why we love
DADS

Kids on Playing Catch,
Piggyback Rides, and Other
Great Things About Dad

Angela Smith &
Jennifer Sander

Adams Media
Avon, Massachusetts

Published by Adams Media, an F+W Publications Company
57 Littlefield Street, Avon, MA 02322. U.S.A.
www.adamsmedia.com

ISBN 10: 1-59337-734-7
ISBN 13: 978-1-59337-734-2

Printed in Canada.

J I H G F E D C B A

Library of Congress Cataloging-in-Publication Data
Smith, Angela.
Why we love dads / Angela Smith and Jennifer Sander.
p. cm.
ISBN-13: 978-1-59337-734-2
ISBN-10: 1-59337-734-7
1. Fathers—Quotations. 2. Children—Quotations. I. Sander, Jennifer Basye. II. Title.

PN6084.F3S65 2007
818'.60208092051—dc22

                            2006102180

This publication is designed to provide accurate and authoritative information with regard to the subject matter covered. It is sold with the understanding that the publisher is not engaged in rendering legal, accounting, or other professional advice. If legal advice or other expert assistance is required, the services of a competent professional person should be sought.
                    —From a *Declaration of Principles* jointly adopted by a Committee of the
                    American Bar Association and a Committee of Publishers and Associations

Many of the designations used by manufacturers and sellers to distinguish their product are claimed as trademarks. Where those designations appear in this book and Adams Media was aware of a trademark claim, the designations have been printed with initial capital letters.

This book is available at quantity discounts for bulk purchases.
For information, please call 1-800-289-0963.

contents

iii

introduction

I have spent many years around young children. My first job was babysitting my three younger cousins. While attending college I worked at a preschool. Finally, I ended up teaching kindergarten while raising my own two sons.

One thing I've noticed through all my years spending time with young children . . . they just say the cutest things. They are so honest, innocent, and impulsive. Be careful, a five-year-old will tell you exactly what he is thinking if you ask.

I hope you enjoy this brief peek into the mind of a kindergartner as you hear how they truly view their parents. Some of the answers will make you smile in recognition, some of them will make you laugh, and some are heartbreaking in their honest emotion.

—*Angela Smith*

i love my dad because...

Why do young children love their dads? As parents, we might assume their reasons are emotional—because we protect them, because we nurture them. Surprise! Who knew that, according to children, it is because, "He has a new beard. Beards are cool," or "He takes me to Starbucks in the morning"? Children are far more practical and clear-eyed than we imagine—keep that coffee coming!

He takes me on my uncle's boat.

Trevor, age 4

He likes to make forts with me in the family room.

Parker, age 5

He helps me get into trees—I love to climb trees!

Cole, age 5

When he comes home from work he gives me hugs and kisses.

Hannah, age 4

He lets me play with Brandon a lot.

Claire, age 7

He plays a lot of games with me.

Kelan, age 5½

He tickles me.

Amanda, age 5

He helps me when I get hurt.

Natalie, age 6

He loves me.

Carson, age 6

He gives me toys when i go to the store.

Michael, age 6

He's the boss of me.

Cade, age 5

He makes stuff for me.

Brooke, age 6

He gives me lots of hugs.

Rose, age 7

He's cool and he has a new beard. Beards are cool.

Carter, age 6

He's the man of the house.

Michael, age 7

He's very nice to me.

Pierce, age 7

I get to play Playstation with him.

Carret, age 6

He helps out with stuff.

James, age 7

He lets me work with him.

Scott, age 7

He takes me to the mall.

Jamie, age 5

We're both in the same family.

Megan, age 6

He's a good daddy. He's nice and he doesn't get mad at me.

Mabelita, age 5

12

He takes me to Starbucks in the morning and that makes me happy. But . . . we have to get up really early.

Grace, age 5

He takes me to McDonalds.

Sterling, age 5

He's helpful. He helps
me ride my bike and
roots to me to do it.

Morgan, age 6

He wrestles with me.

Hunter, age 6

14

He feeds me.

Morgan, age 6

He takes me to the store almost every night.

Casandra, age 6

He makes me happy.

Amber, age 5

He helps me do
my chores.

Jacob, age 5

He makes me jump really
high on the trampoline.

Dalton, age 6

He makes me laugh.

isabella, age 6

He makes me food.

Declan, age 5

When my mom is on trips he snuggles with me.

Dillon, age 5

When I hop out of the tub he dries me with a warm towel.

Michael, age 6

Because he hugs and holds me when i have a bad dream.

Jacy, age 6

He starts my dirt bike for me!

Jabin, age 6

He makes me sausage and eggs on Saturday.

Matthew, age 5

He comes into my class to see all of the things I've made in kindergarten.

Samantha, age 5

He's funny . . . sometimes.

Colton, age 6

He buys me Ring Pop candy.

Colin, age 6

He lets us make projects by ourselves, like a swing.

Garret, age 6

He plays in the pool with me.

Matthew, age 6

He gives me army men.

Max, age 5

He picks me up from school if my auntie doesn't.

Kylie, age 5

When we play basketball he gives me lots of chances.

Kelan, age 6

24

He takes me on "kid dates" and we go get ice cream.

Rachel, age 5

He hugs me every night.

Brandon, age 6

He doesn't yell at me.

Sterling, age 6

He throws me up in the air.

Samantha, age 5

He likes to hang me upside down.

Darlene, age 6

He builds a house for me.

Hannah, age 6

He protects me,
he's really good at it.

Summer, age 6

He really likes me, I think
'cuz I'm really cute.

Sophia, age 5

**I just love him a lot
because he takes
good care of me.
He says a lot of curse
words but I don't
care. He's a good dad.**

Grant, age 8

He plays hide and seek with me.

David, age 5

He's special and he works for money for us.

Alissa, age 5

He lets me play with the big TV.

Matthew, age 5

He makes super good cookies.

Braden, age 5

He takes me to Baskin Robbins for ice cream.

Samantha, age 5

i need my dad because...

Think of a young child's basic needs—warmth, shelter, food, safety. Add to those needs some of the reasons our young respondents need their daddies—to make pancakes for dinner or chili for the family (one boy kindly points out that his mom can't make chili like his dad can). Oh, and if we didn't have dads, then who would mow the lawn, build the houses, and help their kids make breakfast on Mother's Day?

He cooks the meat for us to eat. Without the meat we would die.

Michael, age 7

if my mom is gone he helps me with my saddle.

Maycee, age 5

34

He loves me.

Claire, age 7

If I didn't have a dad how would I get money?

Cole, age 5

He will rescue me if there's an earthquake.

Kelan, age 5½

To save me from robbers.

Amanda, age 5

I like him.

Brandon, age 6

He protects me.

Natalie, age 6

He cooks me yummy breakfasts.

Carson, age 6

I love him.

Michael, age 6

If I scream he will come.

Hannah, age 4

He makes me a lot of money. He makes my allowance.

Cassidy, age 5

He makes a monkey face.

Cade, age 5

He snuggles with me.

Brooke, age 6

He takes good care of me.

Rose, age 7

If I didn't have him I'd be very sad. I can't live without him.

Pierce, age 7

If I didn't had my dad,
I couldn't do a lot of stuff.

James, age 7

**I sit with him at night
and we watch stuff.**

Samantha, age 6

He gives us a house.

Scott, age 7

He helps me do stuff I can't really do.

Adhley, age 6

When my mom is gone he watches me.

Grace, age 5

He helps fix things.

Brennen, age 6

44

He helps me with some things. Like on Mother's Day he helps me make mom breakfast.

Megan, age 6

So he can help me learn.

Jamie, age 5

He helps me fix my toys.

Mabelita, age 5

We always play checkers.

Sterling, age 5

46

He holds me so I don't fall down.

Morgan, age 6

He always plays dress up with me.

Casandra, age 6

He helps me take care of my mom when she's sick.

Amber, age 5

He takes me on camping trips to his camp.

Jacob, age 5

He helps my mom do stuff like do the dishes.

Julia, age 5

He helps me at stuff like jumping on the trampoline.

Dalton, age 6

49

He cooks me dinner when my mom doesn't feel good.

Darlene, age 6

He really likes me.

isabella, age 6

He rides motorcycles with me.

Will, age 6

My mom can't make chili like he can.

Dewey, age 7

He makes the money.

Colin, age 6

He's strong.
He's a lot strong.

Toby, age 5

So he can build us a house.

Garrett, age 6

He picks me up when we fall down after someone pushes me over.

Kylie, age 5

He helps me set up the bat when I'm ready to hit.

Kelan, age 6

He needs me to take care of.

Rachel, age 5

He mows the grass.

Layni, age 8

He makes pancakes
for dinner.

Samantha, age 5

55

He helps me put stuff together, like my toys.

Dalton, age 6

He works. He designs houses and that's a really important job.

Hannah, age 6

He lets me have a dollar to buy something.

Brandon, age 6

He doesn't let anybody get me, like bad guys who have to go to jail.

Summer, age 6

He goes to school for my homework.

Sophia, age 5

He carries me on his back, but sometimes he doesn't because he breaks his back.

Lillieth, age 5

We would not run out of money.

Kevin, age 7

He gives us money to buy stuff.

David, age 5

He can play songs on the guitar.

Maya, age 5

He helps me hit baseballs.

Cade, age 5

When the gutter is broken on my house he can fix it.

Braden, age 5

the funniest thing about my dad is...

Pratfalls and funny faces score big with the kinder-garten set, as do some parental attempts at singing, and using funny voices. Pranks, tickling, and, well . . . passing gas, also strike children as pretty goofy when dad is behind it.

He makes funny faces at me.

Claire, age 7

He's not very good at miniature golf, I have to help him.

Trevor, age 4

When he plays with my dog and makes funny growls.

Natalie, age 6

He plays shark and pretends to eat fishy steaks on my arm.

Maycee, age 5

**He toots
and laughs.**

David, age 5

He dances at me
like a clown.

Michael, age 6

He likes to run up the stairs to the pool and jump in to surprise us.

Hannah, age 4

He pretends to punch my brother.

Brooke, age 6

He drops the elbow on me.

Rose, age 7

He has gas a lot.

Carter, age 6

He lets me tackle him.

Matthew, age 5

He makes flips and he does funny noises when he does.

Braden, age 5

Carries me to bed.

Michael, age 7

He plays colors in the pool with me.

Cassidy, age 5

He says "BONSAI" when he does giant cannonballs.

Pierce, age 7

He likes to throw me up in the air.

Samantha, age 5

He makes jokes.

Samantha, age 6

That he calls baseball a "drop."

Scott, age 7

That he tickles me.

Ashley, age 6

He doesn't wear a shirt to bed only pajama bottoms.

Megan, age 6

He's always crazy. He's a very funny daddy.

Grace, age 5

He says silly words.

Parker, age 6

74

He makes silly sounds with his mouth.

Mabelita, age 5

He always sings in the car.

Zoe, age 5

Sometimes he talks in a funny voice.

Morgan, age 6

When he talks to my baby sister he does it with a baby voice.

Casandra, age 6

When he laughs, he makes me laugh.

Amber, age 5

He tells us funny jokes.

Jacob, age 5

He growls at me.

Dalton, age 6

He only sings songs with me at night, he doesn't pray with me.

Isabella, age 6

He's a weirdo.

Colton, age 6

He tickles us when we pretend to be asleep.

Colin, age 6

He always says
"twinkers." I don't know
what it means, but he
says it when it is a
happy day.

Garret, age 6

He likes to throw me up in the pool.

Matthew, age 6

He farts really loud!

Max, age 5

He pranks me.

Kelan, age 6

When he laughs,
it's on the inside
and his belly jiggles.

Rachel, age 5

the funniest thing about my dad is...

He helps us trick our mom on April Fool's Day.

Darlene, age 6

He does karate.

Brandon, age 6

He still likes to play with toys—a lot.

Jillian, age 6

He likes to sing me songs on the phone.

Sophia, age 5

He says we go to the bathroom like racehorses.

Grant, age 8

He makes bunny ears when my mom is talking on the phone.

Sarah, age 7

when i am a dad i will...

So how will the little boys we talked to do it differently when years from now it is their turn to be a dad? Not surprisingly, many focused not on parenting, but on the fact that they will be able to drive by then! Others were making career plans, hoping to be firefighters and policeman and astronauts. One great advantage to being a dad, it seems, is that you can "have the whole house to myself."

Drive a car.

Joey, age 6

Wrestle with my dad and brother. i'll win. He'll be an old man and barely walk.

Garret, age 5

Go outside and go to work. i'm gonna cut down trees.

Will, age 6

Take care of my children. I will take them to Toys R Us and get me everything they want.

Kelan, age 5

Drive my kids to places.

Declan, age 5

Drive a car and have
a pink and blue house.
One side will be pink and
one side will be blue.

Michael, age 5

Have the whole house to myself.

Brenner, age 6

Go to work.

Parker, age 6

Always say yes to my kids. i think!

Sterling, age 5

Be really good at golfing.

Trevor, age 4

Help my children do their homework every day.

David, age 5

Be a policeman.

Trenton, age 6

Work hard.

Max, age 6

Own a store.

Hunter, age 6

Work on road construction.

Cade, age 5

Bake breakfast and work.

Braden, age 5

Be in the Army.

Carter, age 6

Be with my son all the time. I won't have a job so I could be with him.

Pierce, age 7

Be an astronaut.

Brandon, age 6

Have a job.

Carson, age 6

Teach my kids to dance.

Michael, age 6

Shave and do dad stuff.

Carter, age 6

Take my kids to Alcatraz.

Michael, age 7

Be with my wife if i have a boy or girl or twins.

Pierce, age 7

Be a firefighter.

Scott, age 7

Be a vet and save animals.

Brenner, age 6

Go to Dad Work . . . and help my family do stuff.

Parker, age 6

Get my kids some toys.

Sterling, age 5

Be the boss!

Hunter, age 6

Sing in the choir like my dad.

Jacob, age 5

Get a real job.

Dalton, age 6

Buy a real big motorcycle.

Will, age 6

Design computer games and always let my kids play them.

Jonathan, age 7

Be really nice to all kids.

Matthew, age 6

Watch cartoons with my kids.

Toby, age 5

Drive to the airport so I can fly to Hollywood if my kids want to go.

Kelan, age 6

Be an ice cream worker because my kids will like ice cream.

Dalton, age 6

Be a teacher, I forgot why. But I will be a mom and a soccer player too.

Lillieth, age 5

106

Get to play video games all the time.

Matthew, age 5

Play football.

Declan, age 5

i'm happiest when my dad...

How can you keep a child happy? Sure, toys are always a safe bet, but simple things like wrestling on the floor, hanging around the house, and running the nightly bath score big. Oh, and for really happy children, don't forget to "bring home candy."

Plays with me.

Claire, age 7

When my dad hugs me.

Kelan, age 5½

Plays rough football with me. I like to hit him hard.

Julian, age 10

Does fun stuff with my brother and me.

Zoey, age 7

Remembers to buy the kind of cereal I like.

Jonathan, age 7

Makes the "CLAW" to me.

Brooke, age 6

Gets me food.

Rose, age 7

Entertains me—tells me
jokes, makes me laugh.

Carter, age 6

Doesn't go on business trips.

Pierce, age 7

Does fun stuff like getting money.

Trevor, age 4

114

Does something to help me.

Parker, age 5

Plays the memory game with me.

Alissa, age 5

Lets us tackle him!

Matthew, age 5

Gives me money.

Cole, age 5

i'm happiest when my dad...

Babysits me when my mom goes away.

Cassidy, age 5

Rides horsey with me.

Maycee, age 5

117

Plays tag and we take turns being "it."

David, age 5

Gets stuff down off a high shelf for me.

Cade, age 5

Reads to me before bedtime.

Samantha, age 5

Has a computer that doesn't have any problems.

Pips, age 6

Takes me to bed at night and tucks me in.

Samantha, age 6

Plays the "Maya" song on the guitar.

Maya, age 5

Lets me play baseball with him.

Scott, age 7

Makes doughnuts.

Ashley, age 6

Helps me turn the water on for the tub. I get it too hot.

Brenner, age 6

Lays on the couch with me.

Jamie, age 5

Fixes my bed.

Megan, age 6

Brings me home candy.

Grace, age 5

Brings me good things from his vacation.

Parker, age 6

Is at home.

Mabelita, age 5

Does anything nice.

Sterling, age 5

Takes me for a ride on
his Harley.

Zoe, age 5

Makes a lot money at his bank.

Morgan, age 6

Wrestles with me.

Hunter, age 6

Whittles with me. i have three knives and we whittle together. My sister does it too!

Cade, age 5

Goes rollerskating with me.

Julia, age 5

Makes me laugh by scaring me.

Dalton, age 6

Plays games with me— like the Curious George game.

Isabella, age 6

Lets me ride on the tractor.

Colin, age 6

Buys me a toy parachute.

Garret, age 6

129

Lets me drive the golf cart.

Samantha, age 5

Gets me a Barbie!

Kylie, age 5

Lets me jump on his bed.

Kelan, age 6

Does the barbecue!

Lexie, age 7

Is home with me.

Layni, age 8

He makes special burritos with sour cream!

Cassidy, age 5

Takes me to the mall. I love Teddy Crafters!

Darlene, age 6

Feeds us breakfast.

Hannah, age 6

133

Hugs me and lets me have quarters and stuff.

Brandon, age 6

Plays with my flying airplane.

Jillian, age 6

Comes home from his faraway school.

Sophia, age 5

Says a knock-knock joke about bananas. It makes me laugh, sometimes.

Lillieth, age 5

135

Plays football with me. He's a good football player. One time he hit me in the face.

Grant, age 8

He lets me go to his work.

Kevin, age 7

Reads a book to me at night.

Sarah, age 7

Smiles at me.

Colton, age 6

i'm saddest when my dad...

What makes young children sad? No one likes to be spanked, or yelled at, or left behind when their daddy goes away on business, or on "important, secret trips." Kids would also prefer that their dads not "forget to pick me up from school" or "forget to buy lemonade." Priorities, people!

Is at work 'cuz I miss him.

Trevor, age 4

Doesn't take me hunting.

Parker, age 5

Gets hurt.

Kelan, age 5½

Goes away for a few days.

Amanda, age 5

Talks about the accident he had.

Natalie, age 6

Goes to work for a long time.

Carson, age 6

Won't give me toys.

Michael, age 6

Gets mad at me.

Zoey, age 7

Spanks me.

Cade, age 5

Goes to Mexico without me.

Brooke, age 6

144

Goes hunting on a mountain a long, long way away.

Cole, age 5

Leaves to make pools, it takes a really long time!

Hannah, age 4

Goes far away from my house.

Cassidy, age 5

He went to a work business when a hurricane was happening.

Cassidy, age 5

146

Spanks me when I'm bad.

Michael, age 7

Goes on important, secret trips.

Pierce, age 7

Goes to a wedding with my mom.

Maycee, age 5

Goes on the longest trip ever.

David, age 5

Sends me to my room when my brother does things.

Garret, age 6

Is in a bad mood.

James, age 7

Goes on business trips.

Samantha, age 6

Makes me go to bed.

Scott, age 7

I get in trouble and my dad sends me to my room.

Ashley, age 6

Goes to Florida.

Alissa, age 5

Can't play with me when he's too busy.

Braden, age 5

Dies . . . when he dies I will be sad.

Megan, age 6

Goes to the store without me.

Grace, age 5

Goes to work.

Mabelita, age 5

Yells when I'm in trouble.

Sterling, age 5

Trips or spanks me.

Hunter, age 6

Forgets to buy lemonade.

Dwayne, age 7

**Doesn't pick me up
after school and I
have to go to daycare.**

Morgan, age 6

Has to go a long way away and I can't see him.

Casanara, age 6

Hurts my feelings.

Dalton, age 6

Doesn't pray with me at night.

Isabella, age 6

Goes to work—he works really far away.

Will, age 6

Goes away to a softball game because I miss him.

Declan, age 5

Gets mad. One time he broke one of our chairs.

Colton, age 6

Gets hurt on his bike.

Matthew, age 6

Yells at me when I'm mean to my brother.

Max, age 5

Goes somewhere and forgets to tell us.

Kylie, age 5

Gets cut by a knife and his finger is bloody.

Kelan, age 6

Sends me to time-out when I say "no."

Rachel, age 5

Makes me go to my room because i'm bad.

Brandon, age 6

Goes away to Yakima, Washington, for business.

Lexie, age 7

Sends me to my room when I'm rude at the table.

Darlene, age 6

162

i'm saddest when my dad...

Hammers his hand.

Dalton, age 6

Goes to the hospital.

Hannah, age 6

Has to work late and then i fall asleep before he gets home.

Jillian, age 6

Goes away with my mom to someplace special.

Grant, age 8

Says we can't go to the park or shopping. But when it rains I'm sad because our tent is metal and we can't camp.

Lillieth, age 5

Leaves for work.

Rebecca, age 6

Gets fired.

Kevin, age 7

Has to work out in the heat.

Sarah, age 7

the best thing my dad can do is...

All children believe their dad is the best. Some are the best in the kitchen (Macaroni and cheese! Milk-shakes!), others are champion bike fixers and computer gamers And what dad wouldn't be proud that his child has noticed his dad's ability to run a hundred miles? Keep up the great work, guys!

Make good macaroni & cheese.

Claire, age 7

Pretty much make coffee for my mom.

Kelan, age 5½

the best thing my dad can do is...

Fix the house.

Brandon, age 6

Wrestle with me.

Natalie, age 6

Cook my food.

Carson, age 6

Make a dinosaur with water and slide.

Michael, age 6

Fix my bike.

Brooke, age 6

Give me good night kisses.

Rose, age 7

Make shakes.

Carter, age 6

Go to the park with me.

Michael, age 7

Be my friend.

Pierce, age 7

Run 100 miles.

Garret, age 6

Save a life 'cuz he's a fire fighter.

Scott, age 7

Soccer! He's really good at soccer and he's my coach.

Trevor, age 4

Help me swing.

Parker, age 5

Get a buck with big, big horns.

Cole, age 5

Get money to buy us food so we don't die.

Hannah, age 4

Work. He kinda builds houses. He also takes me on walks.

Cassidy, age 5

176

Cook macaroni or steak.

Maycee, age 5

Play music.

Maya, age 5

Dive for rings in the pool with me.

Alissa, age 5

Give piggy back races.

Matthew, age 5

the best thing my dad can do is...

Fix golf carts.

Braden, age 5

Make his brownies!

Samantha, age 5

Work on the computer.

Megan, age 6

Play Candyland with me.

Grace, age 5

Make paper for us.
He prints it out on his
computer at work.

Parker, age 5

Be nice to people.

Mabelita, age 5

Take me to my friend's house.

Zoe, age 5

Hunt for ducks.

Casandra, age 6

Paint a picture for me.

Amber, age 5

Work to get money so we can get new rooms.

Jacob, age 5

Ride on log rides with
me at Disneyland.

Dalton, age 6

**Do pools.
He's a pool guy!**

Isabella, age 6

the best thing my dad can do is...

Fix my quad.

Will, age 6

Play his software game.

Declan, age 5

Work at the place he's working at.

Colton, age 6

Tractor work. He's a really good worker.

Colin, age 6

Shoot really good with a bow and a gun.

Garret, age 6

Help me when I get hurt.

Matthew, age 6

Throw me really, really high in the pool.

Max, age 5

Take me on vacations to the beach.

Toby, age 5

the best thing my dad can do is...

**Build houses
and stuff like that.**

Kylie, age 5

Make pancakes and
syrup and butter too for
breakfast.

Kelan, age 6

Play chess with me.

Sterling, age 6

Make real meatballs.

Lexie, age 7

Catch animals.

Darlene, age 6

Break boards with his foot.

Brandon, age 6

Makes "pasagna." It's delicious but I only eat the part with no cheese.

Summer, age 6

My dad is best at loving.

Sarah, age 7

Kill wolf spiders 'cuz I'm really scared of them.

Sophia, age 5

Do a headstand and spin.

Forest, age 7

Be a good dad.

Zoey, age 7

Work out.

Hunter, age 6

Fix his toy truck.

Jamie, age 5

Make money. He's the best software person.

Julia, age 5

my dad looks silly when he...

Words to the wise, fathers. If you don't want your children to snicker behind your back, don't act out the "cow shake commercial," or make a monkey face, or put on your sunglasses. Do try to keep your dignity intact at all times.

Dresses in clown clothes.

Claire, age 7

Makes funny faces when we wrestle.

Natalie, age 6

Puts a mask on his face.

Michael, age 6

Pulls his ears and looks like a monkey.

Rose, age 7

Does the cow shake commercial.

Michael, age 7

Scrunches up his face.

Scott, age 7

Puts his underwear on his head.

Brenner, age 6

My dad doesn't really ever look silly. He doesn't do anything.

Megan, age 6

Makes weird sounds.

Parker, age 6

Plays with my hamster.

Mabelita, age 5

Rides my brother's little motorcycle.

Zoe, age 5

Works out. He gets sweaty and makes funny faces like he's in pain.

Hunter, age 6

Plays clapping games with me.

Casandra, age 6

Pretends to be dead and tricks my brother.

Trevor, age 4

Puts his tongue on his nose . . . his tongue is really long!

Parker, age 5

Spikes his hair up.

Cole, age 5

Catches fish and holds them up in the air.

Maycee, age 5

Puts the flashlight on his face and makes faces when his face glows.

David, age 5

Pretends to be weird.

Matthew, age 5

Plays with my dog.

Samantha, age 5

His beard grows. His mustache is black and his beard is all gray!

Pips, age 7

When he makes goofy sounds.

Amber, age 5

my dad looks silly when he...

Laughs at me.

Isabella, age 6

Puts on sunglasses.

Will, age 6

**Sticks his tongue
out at me.**

Colton, age 6

Dresses up in weird
costumes for Halloween.

Garret, age 6

Copies what i'm doing or saying.

Matthew, age 6

Plays hide and seek with me.

Kylie, age 5

Shaves.

Sterling, age 6

Dances and sings to his favorite songs.

Lexie, age 7

Mows the lawn and wears a sombrero.

Layni, age 8

He does a dance when he laughs.

Jillian, age 6

Ran into the glass door.

Sarah, age 7

Makes a face like a goofy clown.

Samantha, age 5

Puts his fingers in his mouth.

Dalton, age 6

Wrestles. He puts his arms up to make big muscles.

Trevor, age 5

Lets my dog walk on top of him.

Sam, age 5

Falls into his bed and bounces.

Brayden, age 5

my dad looks silly when he...

is way too big for his little convertible.

Pips, age 7

Forgets to pull his pants up all the way and they slip a little.

Maycee, age 6

217

Pretends to spank himself.

Cole, age 5

Tries to pour coffee and misses the cup.

Brandt, age 6

Does magic and pulls a ball out of his ear.

David, age 5

Dances.
He shakes his rear.

Parker, age 5

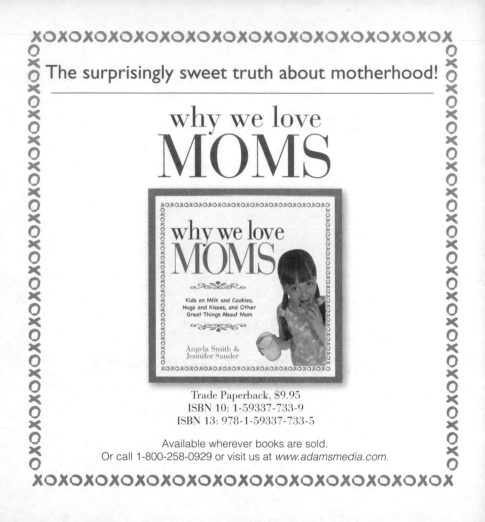